THOMAS HARDY'S

The Withered Arm

Peter Leigh

Published in association with The Basic Skills Agency

Hodder & Stoughton

A MEMBER OF THE HODDER HEADLINE

Acknowledgements
Cover: David Smith
Illustrations: Jim Elderidge
Photograph of Thomas Hardy © Dorset County Mueseum

Orders: please contact Bookpoint Ltd, 130 Milton Park, Abingdon, Oxon OX14 4SB. Telephone: (44) 01235 827720, Fax: (44) 01235 400454. Lines are open from 9.00–6.00, Monday to Saturday, with a 24 hour message answering service. You can also order through our website: www.hodderheadline.co.uk

British Library Cataloguing in Publication Data
A catalogue record for this title is available from The British Library

ISBN 0 340 74307 7

First published 1999
Impression number 10 9 8 7 6 5 4
Year   2004 2003

Typeset by Fakenham Photosetting Limited, Fakenham, Norfolk.
Printed in Great Britain for Hodder & Stoughton Educational, a division of Hodder Headline, 338 Euston Road, London NW1 3BH by The Bath Press, Bath

About the author

Thomas Hardy was born in 1840
and died in 1928.
He lived in the countryside for all his
life, and wrote about country people.
They often had very unhappy lives, and
Hardy wrote about that unhappiness.

About the story

Years ago when this story was written
farmers were rich and important people.
But the men and women who worked for them
were much poorer.

This is the story of one such farmer
and a poor milkmaid.

I

When Farmer Lodge was a young man,
he started seeing
a poor milkmaid called Rhoda Brook,
but although they had a son,
he did not marry her and stopped seeing her.

Twelve years later news came
that Farmer Lodge had got married.
It was all the gossip among the women
doing the milking.

The people speak
with a country
accent.

'He do bring home his bride to-morrow,
I hear.'

'Have anybody seen her?' said another.

'No,' said the first.
'Though they say
she's a rosy-cheeked,

tisty-tosty means
attractive

tisty-tosty little body enough.'

1

This is **Rhoda**.

As the milkmaid spoke she turned her face
so she could glance past the cow's tail
to the other side of the barn
where a thin fading woman of thirty was
milking.

'Years younger than he, they say,'
said the second.

'How old do you call him, then?'

'Thirty or so.'

'More like forty,' broke in an old milkman.
'He was born before our Great Weir
was built,
and I hadn't a man's wages
when I carried water there.'

'Now then,' said the dairyman,
'what does it matter to us
about Farmer Lodge's age,
or Farmer Lodge's new missus?
I shall have to pay him nine pound a year
for the rent of every one of these milchers,
whatever his age or hers.
Get on with your work,
or 'twill be dark afore we have done.
The evening is pinking in already.'

Nothing more was said aloud,
but the first woman murmured
under her cow to her neighbour.

''Tis hard for she,' pointing to Rhoda.

'Oh no,' said the other.
'He hasn't spoke to Rhoda Brook for years.'

When the milking was done
they washed their pails
and hung them on a stand.
They began to go home.
Rhoda was joined by a boy of twelve or so,
and they went away up the field
to a lonely cottage
high above the water-meads.

The **water-meads**
are low-lying fields
next to the river.

'They've just been saying
that your father brings his young wife
home tomorrow,' said Rhoda.
'I shall want to send you
for a few things to market,
and you'll be pretty sure to meet them.'

'Yes, mother,' said the boy.
'Is father married then?'

Rhoda wants to
know what she looks
like.

'Yes ... You can give a look,
and tell me what she's like,
if you do see her.'

'Yes, mother.'

Does she look like a lady, or a working woman like Rhoda?

'If she's dark or fair,
and if she's tall – as tall as I.
And if she seems like a woman
who has ever worked for a living,
or one that has been always well off,
and has never done anything,
and shows the marks of the lady on her.'

Their cottage is very poor.

They crept up the hill in the twilight,
and entered the cottage.
It was built of mud walls,
and here and there in the thatch above
a rafter showed like a bone
sticking through the skin.

Rhoda is still thinking about the young wife.

'Yes,' she said,
'see if she is dark or fair,
and if you can,
notice if her hands be white;
if not, see if they look as though
she had ever done housework,
or are milker's hands like mine.'

The boy promised he would.

II

A **gig** is a small
horse-drawn cart for
two people.

The next evening
while the sun was yet bright,
a handsome new gig,
with a lemon-coloured body and red wheels,
was spinning westward along the highway
at the heels of a powerful mare.
The driver was a farmer in the prime of life.
Beside him sat a woman,
many years younger – almost, indeed, a girl.

The road was empty,
except for one small scarce-moving speck.
It was the boy, creeping on at a snail's pace,
and always looking behind him.
When the gig slowed at the bottom of a hill
the boy was just in front.
He turned,
and looked straight at the farmer's wife
as though he would read her
through and through.

Farmer Lodge knows
who the boy is, but
doesn't say
anything . . .

The farmer,
though he seemed annoyed at the boy,
did not order him to get out of the way.
And so they walked on up the hill,
his hard gaze never leaving her,
till they reached the top,
when the farmer trotted on with relief.

'How that poor lad stared at me!'
said the young wife.

'Yes, dear. I saw that he did.'

... because he hasn't told his wife about him, or about Rhoda.

Gertrude was a popular name at the time of this story.

'He is one of the village, I suppose?'

'Yes. I think he lives with his mother a mile or two off.'

'He knows who we are, no doubt?'

'O yes. You must expect
to be stared at just at first, my pretty Gertrude.'

The farmer drove on.

The boy turned, and went home
to his mother's cottage.

'Well, did you see her?' she asked.

'Yes; quite plain.'

'Is she ladylike?'

'Yes; and more. A lady complete.'

'Is she young?'

'Well, she's growed up,
and her ways be quite a woman's.'

'Of course.
What colour is her hair and face?'

'Her hair is lightish,
and her face as pretty as a live doll's.'

Rhoda wants to
know all the details.

'Her eyes, then, are not dark like mine?'

'No – of a bluish turn,
and her mouth is very nice and red;
and when she smiles her teeth show white.
But why don't you go and see for yourself?'

Rhoda won't go to
see her.
Why not, do you
think?

'I go to see her!
I wouldn't look up at her
if she were to pass my window this instant.'

*And Rhoda would not speak of Gertrude Lodge
again.*

But her thoughts were full of her.

III

At last, tired with her day's work,
Rhoda went to bed.

But the figure that had haunted her
during the day, was not to go away at night.

Gertrude Lodge visited her in her dreams.

Rhoda dreamed that the young wife,
in a pale silk dress and white bonnet,
but with her face horribly twisted
and wrinkled as by age,
was sitting on her chest as she lay;
the blue eyes peered cruelly into her face,
and she thrust forward her left hand
mockingly,
so as to make the ring she wore
glitter in Rhoda's eyes.

The figure in the
dream is showing off
the wedding-ring in
front of Rhoda.

Rhoda struggled, but the figure continued
to flash its left hand as before.

Gasping for breath, Rhoda,
in a last desperate effort,
swung out her right hand,
seized the figure by its left arm,
and whirled it backward to the floor,
starting up herself as she did so
with a low cry.

'O merciful heaven!' she cried,
sitting on the edge of the bed in a cold sweat;
'that was not a dream – she was here!'

She wakes herself
up.

To Rhoda it wasn't
just a dream –
Gertrude seemed to
be really there!

She could feel the figure's arm
within her grasp even now –
the very flesh and bone of it,
as it seemed.
She looked on the floor
where she had thrown the figure,
but there was nothing to be seen.

Rhoda Brook slept no more that night,
and when she went milking at the next dawn

pale and drawn

they noticed how pale and haggard she
looked.
The milk that she drew quivered into the
pail;

The milking was
done by hand, and
her hands were still
trembling.

her hand had not calmed even yet,
and still kept the feel of the arm.
She came home to breakfast
as wearily as if it had been supper-time.

'What was that noise in your room,
mother, last night?' said her son.
'You fell off the bed, surely?'

'Did you hear anything fall? At what time?'

'Just when the clock struck two.'

She could not explain,
and when the meal was done,
went silently about her household work.

Later that morning Gertrude Lodge came visiting.

When Rhoda saw her, she was stunned!
She could not believe
that the figure of her dream
was standing on her front doorstep.
But how different she was!

The figure and the action
were those of the dream:
but her voice was so sweet,
her glance so winning,
her smile so tender,
so unlike the dream,
that Rhoda could hardly believe her eyes.

Remember that **Gertrude**, as a farmer's wife, was an important person in the village, and visiting the poor was one of her duties.

action means the way she moved.

13

Rhoda's heart reproached her bitterly.
This innocent young thing should have
her blessing and not her curse.

'I hope this air agrees with you,' said Rhoda.

Gertrude replied that it did,
her general health being usually good.

'Though now you remind me,' she added,
'I have one little injury which puzzles me.
It is nothing serious, but I cannot make it
out.'

She uncovered her left hand and arm;
it was exactly the same as Rhoda had seen
in her dream.
Upon the pink round surface of the arm
were faint marks of an unhealthy colour,
as if produced by a rough grasp.
Rhoda's eyes became fixed on the marks;
she thought she saw in them
the shape of her own four fingers.

'How did it happen?' she said.

'I cannot tell,' said Gertrude.
'When I was sound asleep,
dreaming I was away in some strange place,
a pain suddenly shot into my arm there,
and was so keen to awaken me.
I must have struck it during the daytime, I
suppose, though I don't remember doing so.'

Gertrude tries to laugh it off, but she is worried by the mark.

She added laughing, 'I tell my dear husband
that it looks just as if he had flown into a
rage
and struck me there.
O, I daresay it will soon disappear.'

'When did it come?'

'When I awoke I could not remember
where I was, till the clock struck two
and reminded me.'

Rhoda started like a guilty thing.

Rhoda thinks she caused the mark even though she didn't want to.

'O, can it be,' she said to herself,
when her visitor had departed,
'that I have an evil power over people
against my own will?'

IV

The summer passed by.

Rhoda tried to avoid Gertrude,
but she kept thinking about her, and her arm.
She wanted to find out if it had got better.

One day she met Gertrude on the road.
She could see that Gertrude
was carrying her arm stiffly.

'I hope your arm is well again,' she said.

'No; it is not quite well.
Indeed it is no better at all;
it is rather worse.
It pains me dreadfully at times.'

'Perhaps you had better go to a doctor.'

She replied that she had already seen a
doctor.
Her husband had insisted on her going to
one.
But the doctor could not understand it;
he had told her to bathe it in hot water,
and she had bathed it,
but the treatment had done no good.

There's no cure.

16

'Will you let me see it?' asked Rhoda.

Gertrude pushed up her sleeve.

As soon as Rhoda saw it,
she could hardly stay calm.
There was nothing like a wound,
but the arm at that point had a shrivelled
look,
and the outline of the four fingers
appeared more distinct than before.

shrivelled means withered, or shrunken

'It looks almost like fingermarks,'
said Gertrude, adding with a faint laugh,
'my husband says it is as if some witch,
or the devil himself,
had taken hold of me there,
and blasted the flesh.'

blasted – means infected, or blighted

Rhoda shivered.
'That's fancy,' she said hurriedly.
'I wouldn't mind it, if I were you.'

here **fancy** means imagination

'I shouldn't so much mind it,'
said Gertrude, with hesitation,
'if – I hadn't a notion that it makes my
husband –
dislike me – no, love me less.
Men think so much of personal appearance.'

notion – means idea

'Some do – he for one.'

'Yes; and he was very proud of mine, at first.'

'Keep your arm covered from his sight.'

'Ah – he knows the marks are there!'
She tried to hide the tears that filled her eyes.

Gertrude is upset not by the hurt, but because her husband likes her less.

'Well, I earnestly hope it will go away soon.'

But it didn't go away.
It became worse,
and as it became worse,
so did Gertrude's unhappiness.

She tried different cures,
but none of them worked.
And then she heard of a healer who lived nearby.
He was called Conjuror Trendle –
'conjuror' because he heals by magic.

Gertrude doesn't really believe in such things,
but she is desperate,
and is willing to try anything.
She persuades Rhoda to come with her
when she visits him.

Conjuror Trendle was at home
when they arrived.
He was a grey-bearded man
with a reddish face,
and he looked oddly at Rhoda
the first moment he saw her.
He examined Gertrude's arm.

'Medicine can't cure it,' he said promptly.
''Tis the work of an enemy.'

Rhoda shrank into herself, and drew back.

'An enemy? What enemy?' asked Gertrude.

He shook his head.
'That's best known to yourself,' he said.
'If you like, I can show the person to you,
though I shall not myself know who it is.
I can do no more;
and don't wish to do that.'

He's unhappy about the whole thing, and doesn't really want anything more to do with it.

But **Gertrude** insists.

She pressed him.
He told Rhoda to wait outside where she
stood,
and took Gertrude into the room.
Rhoda could see through the open door.
He brought a glass from the dresser,
nearly filled it with water,
and broke an egg on the edge of the glass,
so that the white went in and the yolk
remained.

He told Gertrude to watch the mixture
closely.

'Do you catch the likeness of any face or figure as you look?' he said.

She murmured a reply,
and continued to gaze intently into the glass.
Rhoda turned, and walked a few steps away.

When Gertrude came out, her face was very pale.

Trendle shut the door behind her,
and they started at once for home.

Gertrude has seen something.

But Rhoda could see
that Gertrude had quite changed towards
her.

'Did he charge much?' she asked.

'Oh no – nothing. He would not take a
farthing.'

'And what did you see?'

'Nothing I – care to speak of.'

constraint – as if holding herself in

rigid means stiff

The constraint in her manner was
remarkable;
her face was so rigid as to look older,
more like the face in Rhoda's dream.

It was a long and dreary walk home.
The two women said no more to each other.

But in some way or other
a story was whispered about that winter,
that Gertrude's injury was owing to her
being 'overlooked' by Rhoda Brook.

overlooked here means that it is as though **Gertrude** had an evil spell cast over her by **Rhoda**.

Why do you think **Rhoda** moves away?

Rhoda said nothing about it,
but her face grew sadder and thinner;
and in the spring she and her boy
disappeared from the neighbourhood.

V

Six years passed.

Gertrude's marriage became worse and worse.
Her husband spoke to her less and less.
He thought about Rhoda Brook and her son.
He thought that Gertrude's arm was
a judgement from heaven on him
for leaving Rhoda.

Gertrude was now twenty-five,
but she seemed older.

'Six years of marriage,
and only a few months of love,'
she sometimes whispered to herself.
'If only I could be again as he first saw me.'

She went again to see Conjuror Trendle.

'You can send away warts, I know,' she said;
'why can't you send away this?'
And she uncovered her withering arm.

'You think too much of my powers,'
said Trendle; 'and I am old and weak now, too.
No, no; it is too much
for me to attempt in my own person.
There is only one chance of doing it
known to me.
It has never failed – that I can declare.
But it is hard to carry out,
and especially for a woman.'

'Tell me!' said Gertrude.

'You must touch with the arm
the neck of a man who's been hanged.'

She started a little.

'Before he's cold – just after he's cut down.'

'How can that do good?'

improve the health

'It will turn the blood
and change the constitution.
But, as I say, to do it is hard.
You must go to a jail
when there's a hanging,
and wait for him
when he's brought off the gallows.'

Conjuror Trendle was right.
It was hard to do!
To lay your arm across the neck
of a man who has just been hanged!
The thought of it turned Gertrude cold.
But it might work,
it might 'turn the blood',
and then her arm would be healed.

The more she thought about it,
the more it seemed there was no other way.

In those days men were hung
for very minor crimes like horse-stealing or arson,
so it was not long before she heard
that a hanging was due to take place.

Gertrude did not want to tell her husband –
he seemed even more gloomy and silent than
usual –
but the jail was some way away,
and she didn't know how to get there
without letting him know.

arson is setting fire
to buildings on
purpose

*But then he told her
that he had some business to attend to
and would be away for a few days.
It was the chance she was waiting for.*

*After he had gone, she saddled a horse,
and rode to the jail.
She went to the hangman's house,
and knocked on the door.
He answered it.*

'Yes Miss? What do you want here?'

'To speak to you a minute.
What time is the execution?'

In the days of the story, before rail, letters had to be delivered by coach.

'The same as usual – twelve o'clock,
or as soon after as the mail-coach
from London gets in.
We always wait for that
in case of a pardon.'

'Oh – a pardon – I hope not,' said Gertrude
without thinking.

If the man is let off, the hangman won't be paid.

Hayricks were valuable, and they were burnt as a protest because the farmers were rich and everyone else poor. It was very severely punished.

'Well, as a matter of business, so do I!
But still if ever a young fellow deserved
to be let off, this one does;
he was only just present by chance
when the rick was fired.
However, there's not much risk of it,
as they are forced to make an example of
him.'

'I mean,' she explained,
'that I want to touch him for a charm,
a cure for an affliction.'

'Oh yes, miss! Now I understand.
I've had such people come in past years.'

'You can arrange it for me?'

'You can do everything
that's necessary for me?'

'You should really have gone
to the governor of the jail,
and given your name and address –
that's how it used to be done, if I recollect.
Still, perhaps I can manage it for a small fee.'

'Oh thank you! I would rather do it this way, as I should like it kept private.'

'Lover not to know, eh?'

'No – husband,'

'Aha! Very well. I'll get you a touch of the corpse.'

'Where is it now?' she said, shuddering.

'It? He, you mean; he's living yet. Just inside that little window up there.' He pointed to the jail on the cliff above.

She thought of her husband and her friends. 'Yes, of course,' she said. 'What am I to do?'

'Now you be waiting by the little gate in the wall,
that you'll find up there in the lane,
not later than one o'clock.
I will open it from the inside,
as I shan't come home to dinner till he's cut down.
Good night.
Be punctual;
and if you don't want anybody to know you, wear a veil.
Ah, once I had a daughter such as you!'

And he closed the door.

VI

The next day at one o'clock
the little gate in the wall round the jail
was opened,
and Gertrude was let in.

She was wearing a veil,
and her left arm was in a loose sleeve.

In front of her was a rough coffin.

It was open,
and in it was the body of a young man.

By this time the young woman's state was
such
that a grey mist seemed to float before her
eyes,
on account of which, and the veil she wore,
she could scarcely see anything.

'Now!' said a voice close at hand.

She bared her poor cursed arm;
and the hangman,
uncovering the face of the corpse,
took Gertrude's hand, and held it
so that her arm lay across the dead man's
neck,

the marks caused by
the rope

upon a line the colour of an unripe
blackberry,
which surrounded it.

Gertrude shrieked:

as **Conjuror Trendle**
had said

'the turn of the blood' had taken place
just like the conjuror had said.

tore through the air

But at that moment
a second shriek rent the air:
it was not Gertrude's,
and its effect upon her
was to make her turn round.

Immediately behind her stood Rhoda Brook,
her face drawn, and her eyes red with
weeping.
Behind Rhoda stood Farmer Lodge;
his face lined, his eyes dim, but without a
tear.

'Damn you! What are you doing here?'
he said hoarsely.

'Hussy – to come between us and our child
now!' cried Rhoda.
'This is the meaning
of what Satan showed me in the vision!
You are like her at last!'

And clutching the bare arm of the younger
woman, she pulled her unresistingly back
against the wall.
Immediately Rhoda let go, the fragile young
Gertrude slid down against the feet of her
husband.
When he lifted her up, she was unconscious.

The hanged man was Rhoda's son.
She and Farmer Lodge were there
to collect the body of their child.
That was 'the business he had to attend to'.

A doctor was called for Gertrude.
She was taken out of the jail into the town;
but she never reached home alive.

Her delicate health,
sapped perhaps by the paralysed arm,
collapsed under the double shock
that followed the severe strain,
physical and mental,
which she had been under
during the previous twenty-four hours.

Her blood had been 'turned' indeed – too far.

Her funeral took place in the town three days
after.

Farmer Lodge was never seen
in the area again.
He sold up everything, and lived alone
in another town.
He died two years later.

sapped means
weakened

Rhoda could not be found,
but reappeared many years later at the dairy.
She took up her old job of milkmaid.
She did this until her body
became bent with age
and her hair white.

People who knew her story
would watch her silently milking a cow,
and wonder what thoughts
must be going through her head.

But she never told.